The Alamo

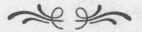

SHIRLEY RAYE REDMOND

ILLUSTRATED BY DOMINICK SAPONARO

ALADDIN PAPERBACKS

New York   London   Toronto   Sydney

For George and Rose Niederauer,
who provided the lovely writer's retreat
—S. R. R.

For my grandfather, George W. Marshall.
80 billion thank-yous. —D. S.

First Aladdin Paperbacks edition May 2004
Text copyright © 2004 by Shirley Raye Redmond
Illustrations copyright © 2004 by Dominick Saponaro

ALADDIN PAPERBACKS
An imprint of Simon & Schuster Children's Publishing Division
1230 Avenue of the Americas, New York, NY 10020

Also available in an Aladdin Library edition.
Designed by Debra Sfetsios
The text of this book was set in Cheltenham.

Printed in the United States of America
2 4 6 8 10 9 7 5 3 1

Library of Congress Control Number 2003110502
ISBN 0-689-85821-3

You ask me do I remember it, I tell you, Yes. It is burned into my brain and indelibly seared there. Neither age nor infirmity could make me forget, for the scene was one of such horror that it could never be forgotten.

—Enrique Esparza,
who witnessed and survived
the siege when he was
eight years old, son of
slaughtered Alamo defender
Gregorio Esparza

CHAPTER ONE

"Play the Turtle"

THE TEXAS colonists were angry—very angry. In September of 1835 more than thirty thousand Americans were living in Texas. They called themselves "Texians."

For a long time they had been urging Andrew Jackson, president of the United States, to buy the vast territory from Mexico. They desperately wanted to be free from the country's heavy taxes and unfair laws.

Many of the men who immigrated to Texas were sons and grandsons of soldiers who had fought the British redcoats in the American Revolution.

Like the patriots of 1776, the Texas colonists felt oppressed by high taxes and a lack of representation in government. Rebellion was in the air, and the Texians felt their cause was just.

But Mexico's president, General Antonio López de Santa Anna, turned a deaf ear to the settlers' complaints. And he did not want to sell Texas to the United States. He was concerned only with ruling it and the rest of Mexico's vast territories with the iron grip of a dictator.

After being elected president in 1833, Santa Anna took over the government in Mexico City. He abolished the Mexican constitution of 1824. He dissolved the congress and forced the legislators to go home. Mexico was no longer a free democracy. Santa Anna had declared himself absolute ruler of the country!

As dictator, Santa Anna enforced high taxes and harsh laws. He ordered large import fees to be charged for all goods shipped into his country from the United States. He demanded that all citizens give up their guns and rifles.

Santa Anna also enforced an old Spanish law that prohibited American immigrants from coming over the border into Texas. Anyone who did would be considered a pirate . . . and treated like an outlaw! Those who protested were immediately arrested. Santa Anna even sent soldiers into Texas to see that the laws were enforced.

But many of the American colonists in Texas had become citizens of Mexico. Men like Stephen Austin, Jim Bowie, and Ben Milam had taken the oath of loyalty to the Mexican government. They paid their taxes. They joined the Catholic Church, which all

Mexican citizens were required to do. The colonists built homes and towns for their families. Their businesses thrived.

Now their rights as Mexican citizens were being ignored. It wasn't fair! At first the Texians hired lawyers, like Sam Houston and young William Travis, to take their case to court. This took a long time, and the judges did not want to anger the hot-tempered El Presidente in Mexico City.

As time passed the Texians became more frustrated. It was apparent that the Mexican government did not care about the rights of its citizens in the Texas territory. The Mexican constitution of 1824 had allowed Texas to govern itself as the colony grew. Santa Anna, however, had abolished that constitution.

Some of the Texians, including Stephen Austin, banded together to form the Peace Party. They wanted to solve their problems through the courts. They did not want to start a war.

Austin advised the three hundred Americans in his Texas settlement to "play the turtle, hands and feet within our own shells."

Other Texians, like Sam Houston, William Travis, and Jim Bowie, wanted to fight. They were members of the War Party. They formed a militia and encouraged their fellow Texians to revolt against the Mexican government.

Many *Tejanos* also rebelled against Santa Anna's dictatorship. *Tejanos* were Hispanics living in Texas. Erasmo Seguín and José Navarro disapproved of Santa Anna's despotic government.

Juan Seguín, Erasmo's son, formed a troop of armed *Tejanos* to attack Santa Anna's soldiers when they came to collect taxes and arrest troublemakers. Soldiers like José Losoya deserted the Mexican army to join

Seguín's company of freedom fighters.

Lorenzo de Zavala became one of the most important *Tejano* leaders. He was a doctor. He was also Mexico's ambassador to France. When Zavala learned that Santa Anna had abolished the democratic government of Mexico and declared himself dictator, Zavala resigned as ambassador and left Paris immediately.

He traveled to Texas to urge Texians and *Tejanos* to work together to reform the corrupt government in Mexico City. But Santa Anna would not relent. Eventually Zavala joined the Texians in their fight for independence.

Trying to avoid war, Stephen Austin traveled to Mexico City to meet with President Santa Anna. He was kept waiting for months. When he was finally granted a short meeting, President Santa Anna, dressed in flowing lace and glittering military medals, smiled and nodded his head but said he could promise nothing.

Austin fumed. He realized that Santa Anna would never let Texans govern themselves. He wrote a letter to the town council of San Antonio de Bexar declaring that "if people of Texas do not take their affairs into their hands, that land is lost."

He encouraged Texians to unite and declare their independence from Mexico.

A copy of this letter found its way into Santa Anna's hands. The dictator arrested Austin and put him in prison. Austin was in solitary confinement for almost a year.

He was not allowed to see anyone. He had no one to talk to, except for a mouse that he taught to eat from his hand. When Austin was finally released and allowed to return to Texas, he was hailed as a hero.

Peaceful attempts had failed. Now was the

time to fight. Austin, Sam Houston, Lorenzo de Zavala, and others discussed drafting a declaration of independence—in English and Spanish. Houston was chosen to head up the army of Texas.

When Santa Anna learned of the brewing Texas revolution, he ordered his brother-in-law, General Martín Perfecto de Cos, to take troops to Texas to maintain discipline. He also ordered him to arrest some of the worst troublemakers, like William Travis and Zavala.

Word of troops coming spread like wildfire from one Texas settlement to another. And those troops were under orders to arrest the revolutionaries!

Texians quickly armed themselves. With grim determination they all agreed that General Cos would *not* be allowed to arrest anyone!

"Who Will Go with Old Ben Milam?"

DURING THE months of October and November 1835 the Texians organized both a government and an army. Leaders like Sam Houston, Stephen Austin, Juan Seguín, and Lorenzo de Zavala united citizens of the War Party and the Peace Party for the greater good of Texas.

Daring scouts like Deaf Smith kept them informed about the movements of General Cos and the Mexican army.

Jim Bowie, who was made an honorary colonel in command of the Texian volunteers, slipped into enemy camps to count the numbers of men and weapons. Disguised and speaking fluent Spanish, Bowie was never caught!

In this way the settlers at Gonzales learned that Cos was sending troops to take their six-pound cannon. The Mexican government had given the cannon to the Gonzales settlers many years earlier. It was to be used to fend off raiding Indians. Now government troops were coming to take it back.

The Texians decided not to let them have it! They loaded the cannon and were prepared to fire it if necessary. They even hung a banner over the big gun. It taunted, COME AND TAKE IT!

In the town of Goliad a group of forty Texians hacked their way into the military outpost using axes. They disarmed the Mexican soldiers and claimed all the weapons, cannons, and provisions for "the cause."

When his soldiers sheepishly reported that Texians had taken over Goliad, Cos was furious! He was even angrier—but not surprised—to learn that the leader of the attack had been that traitor Ben Milam.

Benjamin Rush Milam grew up in Kentucky. Like many other Americans who immigrated to Mexico, Milam became a Mexican citizen. He even joined the Mexican army in 1824 and served as an officer.

Then President Santa Anna abolished Mexico's democratic government in 1833. Outraged, Milam protested against this move. He was immediately arrested and sent to a prison in Monterrey, Mexico.

But Milam escaped and fled to Texas. There he joined up with Texians fighting for their independence from Santa Anna's despotic rule.

When General Cos set up his headquarters

in San Antonio de Bexar, Milam urged the Texians to take back the town before winter set in. *Tejano* leader Juan Seguín strongly agreed.

Many others weren't so sure. After all, the Mexican general had a large, well-trained army. The soldiers had taken over the entire town with its three thousand residents. The Mexicans were even occupying the old abandoned mission nicknamed the Alamo. They had cannons and plenty of ammunition.

Stephen Austin had gone on a fund-raising trip to the United States. Sam Houston, elected as commander in chief of the Texas army, was away taking care of personal business.

"Maybe we should wait," the more cautious citizens advised.

But Milam said it was important to take back the town as soon as possible. He gave a speech to rally the men and cried out,

"Who will go with old Ben Milam into San Antonio?"

Three hundred volunteers answered his call. Colonel Edward Burleson, who'd been elected to take over the command of the army while Austin and Houston were away, eventually joined him, bringing another five hundred men.

The Texians and Juan Seguín's company of *Tejanos* attacked San Antonio de Bexar at dawn on December 5, 1835. They fought fiercely from house to house and boldly out in the middle of the streets.

No door was strong enough to keep them out. When necessary, the Texians used battering rams. The frontier riflemen on the rooftops scored hundreds of casualties with their amazing accuracy.

General Cos was stunned. The tireless

Texians seemed to be everywhere at once! Pinned down and cut off, with no hope of reinforcements, General Cos meekly surrendered on December 9.

The Texians cheered when they saw the white flag fluttering above the walls of the old mission. But brave Ben Milam did not live to see the victory. He'd been shot in the head by a Mexican sniper and had died instantly—on the very first day of the battle.

Generous in their triumph, the Texians accepted Cos's surrender and took no prisoners. Nor did they shoot any of the captured Mexican soldiers.

Colonel Burleson released General Cos and his troops. He demanded only that they cross the Rio Grande and return to Mexico. They also forced the general and his men to pledge never to violate the Mexican constitution of 1824. Cos signed the treaty.

The Texians allowed the wounded soldiers to stay in San Antonio de Bexar until they were well enough to march back to Mexico.

As it was almost Christmas, soldiers and volunteers with families in Texas were allowed to return home for the holiday.

Men who chose to remain, like William Travis, set up camp inside the Alamo walls. Their tasks were to make sure Cos's men did not turn back into Texas and to see that the wounded Mexicans caused no trouble in town.

It was Christmas Day when General Cos and the remainder of his bedraggled troops arrived home. Embarrassed, Cos told his brother-in-law what had taken place in San Antonio de Bexar.

President Santa Anna was furious . . . and his holiday celebration ruined!

"Such rebellion will not be tolerated!" he declared.

Santa Anna felt personally insulted by Cos's defeat at the hands of those ruffians. He also feared this failure to maintain law and order in Texas would tarnish his own reputation as a soldier.

Then and there he made a fervent vow to punish those Texian rebels himself!

CHAPTER THREE

"Be Always Sure You're Right— Then Go Ahead"

MEANWHILE, THE news of the Texians' plight traveled across the United States. The fight for liberty appealed to men as far away as Maryland, Massachusetts, New Jersey, New York, Pennsylvania, Rhode Island, and Vermont.

The majority of volunteers, however, came from Texas's nearest neighbors, the U.S. southern states, such as North and South Carolina, Georgia, Louisiana, Mississippi, and Alabama. Tennessee and Virginia boasted the largest number of men to fight and die defending the Alamo.

Perhaps it is not surprising that so many of these fearless volunteers had patriotic names, like Patrick Henry Herndon, George Washington Cottle, Andrew Jackson Harrison, and George Washington Main.

But several of the Alamo defenders weren't Americans at all. Twelve were immigrants from Ireland, and another twelve were from England. Four came from Scotland, two from Germany, and one man each from Denmark and Wales.

Davy Crockett was the most famous volunteer to take up arms for Texas. Crockett was already an American legend when he arrived in San Antonio de Bexar with Old Betsy, his trusty flintlock rifle.

Crockett was a skilled sharpshooter and hunter. Wearing a hat made from the fur of a raccoon, he was the most well known

American woodsman since Daniel Boone. He could entertain listeners for hours with his lively tall tales.

Many popular books had already been written about Crockett's adventures. Most of the stories weren't true, but people liked to read them anyway.

Crockett was also a former U.S. congressman. He represented the voters from the state of Tennessee, and his political exploits in Washington, D.C., made for lively newspaper headlines.

When he lost his race for reelection in the fall of 1835, Crockett decided to leave home to fight a different sort of campaign. Although he was no longer a young man, Crockett wanted to help the Texians fight for their liberty.

Crockett lived by a personal motto: "Be

always sure you're right—then go ahead." He was certain that the Texians were doing the right thing.

With a small company of volunteers from his home state of Tennessee, Davy Crockett made his way to Texas, arriving at San Antonio de Bexar in early February 1836. He was impressed with the territory and wrote home about it: "I must say as to what I have seen in Texas it is the garden spot of the world. The best land . . . I ev'r saw and I do believe it is a fortune to any man to come here. . . . I have taken the oath of government and have enrolled my name as a volunteer from the United States. . . . I had rather be in my present situation than to be elected to a seat in Congress for life."

Like Crockett and his flintlock, Jim Bowie and his knife were already famous before he took command of volunteers at the Alamo. Most Texians knew stories about the duels he'd fought and the brawls he'd won, wielding that fearsome knife that his brother Rezin had designed.

Jim Bowie grew up in the Louisiana swamps with his brothers and their parents. They learned to speak Spanish and French as well as English. Cajun youngsters taught the Bowie brothers to rope and ride alligators— and the boys were good at it too!

Bowie was a big man, but a warmhearted one. Those who knew Jim admitted that although he never ran from a fight, he never started one either.

Bowie always had a soft spot for the underdog. In church one Sunday a group of rowdies loudly heckled the small, soft-spoken preacher.

Standing up, Bowie announced, "I'll use

my knife on the next man who interrupts the preacher. And my name is Bowie. Jim Bowie."

Not one man made a peep after that!

Bowie came to Texas to buy and sell land. Besides being gutsy and good natured, he was also a keen businessman. He'd already made a small fortune from slaves, sawmills, and sugar plantations.

Once in Texas, Bowie became a Mexican citizen and joined the Roman Catholic Church. He married Ursula de Veramendi, the beautiful young daughter of an important official in the Mexican government.

Bowie made friends with the Comanches, was adopted by the Apaches, and even financed a risky search for a long-lost Spanish silver mine.

He tried to ignore the growing hostilities between Texas and Mexico. After all, he was a well-to-do Mexican citizen with a Mexican wife and family.

But when push came to shove, Bowie sided with the Texians. He knew all too well that by taking up arms against President Santa Anna, he would be hanged as a traitor if caught.

Bowie accepted that risk. When the Texians successfully captured San Antonio de Bexar and sent General Cos and his humiliated men back to Mexico, Bowie wrote a letter to Sam Houston: "The salvation of Texas depends in great measure on keeping [San Antonio de] Bexar out of the hands of the enemy. . . . If it was in the possession of Santa Anna, there is no stronghold from which to repel him in march. . . . Colonel Neill and myself have come to the solemn resolution that we will rather die in these ditches than give them up to the enemy."

* * * *

William Travis was a young, unknown lawyer from South Carolina. He journeyed to Texas by wagon train and settled in the town of Anahuac. He opened a law office there.

Many of his clients were American settlers with disputes against the Mexican government. Travis felt the court system was unfair. There were too many closed-door sessions with no juries.

Travis was also riled to anger by the military persecution of settlers in the area. Soon Mexican soldiers were sent to Anahuac to collect sky-high duties from the overtaxed colonists. Travis ran out of patience. This time he took the law into his own hands.

In June of 1835 he led a company of armed Texian volunteers against the garrison in Anahuac. Travis confiscated the weapons and ran the frightened soldiers out of town.

Travis was no longer willing to pursue justice in the courtroom. Along with other like-minded Texians, he continued to harass officials of the Mexican government in Texas. He captured cannons and military supplies. He disarmed soldiers and forced them to march out of Texas.

Although some Texians and *Tejanos* regarded Travis as an American hothead, he didn't care. In a letter to Jim Bowie before the battle at the Alamo, Travis declared his loyalty to the Texians' fight for freedom: "Right or wrong, sink or swim, live or die . . . I am with them!"

CHAPTER FOUR

The Napoléon of the West

ANTONIO LÓPEZ de Santa Anna had been a soldier all of his life. At the age of sixteen he was already a cadet in Spain's royalist army. During Mexico's war for independence Santa Anna fought for the Spanish. Later, when it was to his advantage, he switched sides!

Santa Anna loved the smell of gunpowder. He enjoyed giving orders and having them obeyed. He thrived on the excitement of battlefield campaigns. He was ambitious, hot tempered, and proud.

Over the years he earned the reputation of being a tiger on and off the battlefield. He liked to call himself the Napoléon of the West. His enemies nicknamed him Attila of the South, after one of history's most brutal warriors, Attila the Hun.

Santa Anna soon decided that being a popular military hero was not enough. He wanted political power too. With the same ruthless tactics he used on the battlefield, Santa Anna aimed for the presidential palace in Mexico City.

He fought a winning campaign. On April 1, 1833, Santa Anna was sworn in as president of Mexico. He had been the people's over-whelming choice.

Once he moved into the presidential palace, however, Santa Anna realized that being El Presidente was not enough. He wanted to be the absolute ruler of the country!

With careful scheming, he appointed his

friends, relatives, and political supporters to important government positions. With the army under his command, Santa Anna abolished the constitution of 1824 and dissolved the congress of Mexico. By the time he took over the country, no one in Mexico could effectively oppose Santa Anna's dictatorship.

Still, there were outbreaks of rebellion. Frequent revolutions were the normal state of affairs in Mexico. Santa Anna was not overly concerned about those who criticized his regime. He simply had them thrown in prison or hanged.

In May 1835 revolutionaries in the city of Zacatecas rose against him. Santa Anna sent his troops to burn and loot the city. He also ordered the massacre of 2,500 men, women, and children. Such "discipline" was necessary, he insisted. Rebellion must not be tolerated.

But there was something different about the Texians. They wouldn't give up. They resisted arrest. They seized government cannons. They clashed with the soldiers sent to collect unpaid duties and taxes.

In November 1835 the Texians had even held a political convention of sorts. Following this event the Texian leaders issued the Declaration of the People of Texas in General Convention Assembled.

It was published in English and in Spanish, and stated:

WHEREAS, General Antonio Lopez de Santa Anna and other Military Chieftains have, by force of arms, overthrown the Federal Institutions of Mexico, and dissolved the Social Compact which existed between Texas and other Members of the

Mexican Confederacy—Now, the good People of Texas, availing themselves of their natural rights, SOLEMNLY DECLARE . . . that they have taken up arms in defence of their Rights and Liberties, which were threatened by the encroachments of military despots, and in defence of the Republican Principles of the Federal Constitution of Mexico of eighteen hundred and twenty-four.

Determined to teach the defiant Texians a lesson, General Santa Anna carefully planned a sneak attack. The Texians would not expect him to make the long march in midwinter.

His spies reported that many of the Texians and their *Tejano* allies had gone home to their families. The rebels obviously felt secure in their victory at San Antonio de Bexar.

By January of 1836, Santa Anna had raised an army of six thousand soldiers. He intended to march his army to the Rio Grande, then have his men cross the river on rafts.

Santa Anna planned to bring only the most necessary provisions. He did not want the army's advance to be slowed by too many supply wagons and pack mules. He would feed his men by seizing private property along the way.

Vast deserts stretched across the horizon between Mexico City and San Antonio de Bexar. Obtaining enough drinking water for men and animals would be a problem. Santa Anna warned his troops at the beginning that they would be allowed only half rations on the long march.

Santa Anna ordered General Cos to come with the troops under his command. But Santa Anna's brother-in-law reminded El Presidente that as part of his surrender agreement he'd promised never to bear arms against the Texians again.

"I gave my word," Cos told him.

"Nonsense!" Santa Anna declared with a scowl. "Prepare to march to San Antonio."

Putting down the Texas rebellion was now a matter of honor for him. Santa Anna could not forgive that band of ragtag volunteers for publicly embarrassing his brother-in-law at San Antonio de Bexar. He vowed to destroy the Alamo and all her rebellious defenders.

One of the first things he intended to do upon arriving in San Antonio de Bexar was to fly the bloodred banner from the top of San Fernando Cathedral, high above the town. At the sight of the red flag all would know that El Presidente would offer no mercy, no quarter for the rebels.

In his fury Santa Anna even bragged that he would keep marching from Texas straight to Washington, D.C. Once there, he planned to raise the Mexican flag over the Capitol of the United States—right under the nose of that interfering President Jackson!

The president of Mexico made a long list of brutal plans. He wanted to see Jim Bowie hang! The scoundrel was no gentleman, even if he had married into the prestigious Veramendi family. It would be a pleasure to put an end to him and an end to all those fantastic stories about Bowie and his wretched knife!

Santa Anna also planned to arrest Lorenzo de Zavala, his former ambassador, for treason. He would arrest that hot-blooded troublemaker William Travis, too.

His hatred also burned against Erasmo Seguín and his son Juan. Both men were powerful advocates for Texas independence. Juan Seguín had formed a band of *Tejanos* to fight alongside Colonel Burleson, Ben Milam, and Travis.

Seguín had even taken part in the humiliating defeat of General Cos in San Antonio de Bexar. Such rebellion would no longer be tolerated!

The only good thing that had come of that humiliating conflict was the death of the traitor Ben Milam. Santa Anna vowed that all the rebels would meet the same fate. He announced to his officers that this would be a "take no prisoners" campaign.

Every rebel, Texian and *Tejano*, would be put to the sword!

CHAPTER FIVE

"Victory or Death!"

BUT EVEN the Texas weather seemed to defy General Santa Anna. His carefully planned sneak attack failed. It rained so hard that his troops could barely tramp through the slick, heavy mud that Texians called Texas gumbo. Then it snowed.

Many of the Mexican soldiers fell ill from drinking polluted water and died on the march. The horses and pack mules became ill too. Many collapsed on the rugged journey.

Finally President Santa Anna and his government troops arrived on the outskirts of San Antonio de Bexar in late February. He sent scouts to assess the situation in town.

Although disappointed, Santa Anna was not surprised when his men returned with the news. He could see the smoke of cooking fires behind the walls of the fortified mission. He scowled when he saw the flag that flew so defiantly above the Alamo.

It was a Mexican flag, but the number 1824 had been sewn over the top of the tricolor bars. The bold numbers stood for the year the Mexicans had obtained their hard-earned liberty from Spain . . . and adopted a democratic constitution. That was the same constitution that Santa Anna had abolished when he declared himself dictator!

So the Texian rebels were expecting them, it seemed. They were barricaded inside the crumbling one-hundred-year-old mission. They had water, corn, and cattle. They also had defensive cannons in place and ammunition. The troublesome Texians were prepared for a siege.

Santa Anna sent his chief aide, Colonel Juan Almonte, to order the rebels to surrender at once.

Despite the grim odds against them, Colonel Travis responded to the courier's message with cannon fire!

Santa Anna clenched his jaw. The Texians could defy him, but they would *not* defeat him. With fierce determination he launched his well-planned attack.

Colonel Travis had done everything possible to strengthen his position. A sympathetic *Tejano* scout had brought grim news before the siege that *thousands* of Mexican soldiers were seen crossing the Rio Grande at Laredo.

Travis knew the Alamo defenders would not be able to hold out for long. After all, the

Alamo was a mission, not a fortress. It had not been built to hold back an army of thousands.

Once the siege began, Santa Anna's artillery bombardment was constant and destructive. Then the cavalry arrived, swelling the Mexican forces to even larger numbers. Santa Anna's men fired their cannons by day and launched sneak attacks at night. The weary Texians slept and ate at their posts. They kept their muzzleloaders and tomahawks by their sides at all times.

Travis wisely put Davy Crockett and his Tennessee sharpshooters in charge of defending the weakest section of the wall.

Legend has it that Crockett and Old Betsy were the first to draw blood once the attack began. When daring Mexican soldiers inched their way forward, attempting to breach the wall, Crockett and his frontiersmen picked them off one by one.

Then Jim Bowie collapsed with a raging fever. Before joining the thirty other sick men sheltered in the chapel, Bowie placed Travis in charge of the volunteers. This meant Travis was now in sole command of the Alamo. This time there was no bickering between the Texian regulars and Bowie's fiercely loyal volunteers.

On February 24, 1836, a worried Travis wrote a letter urgently appealing for help. It read:

To the People of Texas and all Americans in the world:

I am besieged by a thousand or more of the Mexicans under Santa Anna. I have sustained a continual bombardment and cannonade for 24 hours and have not lost a man. The enemy has demanded a surrender at discretion, otherwise the garrison are to be put to the sword if the fort is taken. I have answered the demand with a cannon shot and our flag still waves proudly from the walls. I shall never surrender or retreat.

Then I call on you in the name of liberty, of patriotism and of everything dear to the American character to come to our aid with all dispatch. The enemy is receiving reinforcements daily and will no doubt increase to three or four thousand in four or five days.

If this call is neglected, I am determined to sustain myself as long as possible and die like a soldier who never forgets what is due to his own honor and that of our country. Victory or Death!

* * * *

Albert Martin volunteered for the risky task of delivering the letter to the town of Gonzales. Travis chose James Butler Bonham to ride to Goliad for help. Scouts had learned earlier that Colonel James Fannin was in command of two hundred Texian volunteers near Goliad. The settlement was nearly one hundred miles away, but Bonham was willing to take the chance.

Hard-riding Juan Seguín was also sent for help. Travis hoped Seguín's fluent Spanish would get him past the Mexican patrols if Martin and Bonham were captured. From his sickbed Bowie urged Seguín to take his horse.

Sharpshooters manned the Alamo walls, giving constant rifle cover so the brave messengers could escape past the Mexican patrols.

Martin successfully delivered Travis's letter.

Copies of the letter made their way across Texas and even into some of the southern states. The hearts of Americans and *Tejanos* alike were deeply touched by Travis's noble words. Many armed themselves and headed for the Alamo.

Thirty-two courageous volunteers from the Gonzales settlement quickly mounted up and followed Martin back to the Alamo.

These volunteers were under the command of Captain George Kimball. They knew from Martin's report what the situation at the Alamo was like. They knew, too, that the odds of winning the battle against Santa Anna were slim.

Bonham returned to the Alamo with a heavy heart. He'd ridden hundreds of miles in five desperate days. Colonel Fannin was *not* coming. Fannin had even told Bonham not to return to the Alamo, that it would be suicide to do so.

But Bonham *did* return. Travis was his friend. They'd grown up together in South Carolina. He felt it was his duty to tell Travis face-to-face that there would be no reinforcements from Goliad.

CHAPTER SIX

"The Loss Is a Small Affair"

March 6, 1836

Day Thirteen of the Siege

IT WAS early in the morning and still dark when General Santa Anna gave the signal to attack. Four columns of soldiers—nearly eighteen hundred men—moved quickly toward the walls of the little mission.

A bugler played "El Degüello." It was a battle tune well known to soldiers. The title means "throatcutting." Perhaps the weary Texans shuddered when they heard the

menacing melody. It meant the Mexicans were determined to kill them all.

The Alamo defenders braced themselves for the brutal assault. Skilled riflemen killed scores of Mexicans with amazing speed and accuracy. Those in the artillery manned the smoking cannons without ceasing.

Twice the outnumbered Texans forced the Mexicans to retreat. But on the third attempt the Mexican army breached the wall. They streamed over the top and into the plaza, shouting victory.

William Travis was one of the first to die from a single shot to the forehead. Twenty-eight-year-old Albert Martin, who had risked his life to deliver Travis's famous letter, was also killed.

Gregorio Esparza, a member of Juan Seguín's company of *Tejanos*, died manning one of the Alamo's cannons. Juan Abamillo and Juan Badillo died with him, as did brave James Butler Bonham, who had returned to the Alamo to die with his friends.

Before he was killed, rifleman José Losoya made sure his wife and children were safely hidden in the chapel.

During the battle sixteen-year-old Galba Fuqua, of French Huguenot descent, stumbled toward Susanna Dickinson. He tried to tell her something, but his jaw had been shattered by a bullet and he couldn't speak. Fuqua, only three days short of his seventeenth birthday, dropped dead at the woman's feet.

William King, a courageous volunteer from Gonzales, died that morning. His father had enlisted in the relief force first, but William convinced him to stay behind to take care of the family. William then signed up to go to the Alamo in his father's place. He was only fifteen years old.

Anthony Wolf, a member of the Texan artillery, begged his slayers to spare his two young sons. But the boys, ages eleven and twelve, were killed anyway, despite their father's dying plea.

Dolphin Floyd, from Gonzales, was slain early in the siege—on the very morning of his thirty-second birthday. An English shoemaker named Marcus Sewell, another settler from Gonzales, was killed too, as was young Charles Zanco, from Denmark, who had only recently come to Texas looking for a new life.

An unidentified black woman was shot and killed between two cannons near the Alamo's crumbling wall.

John, an African-American slave belonging to store owner Francis Desauque, died defending the Alamo.

Sergeant Major Hiram James Williamson,

from Philadelphia, was the highest-ranking enlisted man to die at the Alamo.

As the endless surge of soldiers streamed over the wall, the surviving Texans fled to the dark rooms of the barracks. There they prepared for brutal hand-to-hand combat.

Surgeon Amos Pollard was killed while trying to protect his sick and wounded patients in the barracks. One of these patients was Jim Bowie. Bowie was so ill that he could barely rise from his cot. Eyes glazed with fever, Bowie still managed to fight. He did not die easy. Bowie was shot several times and bayoneted without mercy before he finally collapsed.

Carlos Espalier, Jim Bowie's seventeen-year-old ward, was also killed.

When the Mexicans battered down the chapel doors, they discovered several Texans inside making a last stand to protect the women and children. Some historians say that Davy Crockett was one of these men.

The soldiers marched the prisoners before Santa Anna. The general frowned angrily when he saw them. He became even angrier when his officers asked him to spare the men's lives.

"In this war, you understand, there are *no prisoners,*" he sternly reminded them. Immediately the unarmed Texans were bayoneted. Then they were shot.

One of Santa Anna's lieutenants, José Enrique de la Peña, wrote in his diary that "these unfortunates died without complaining and without humiliating themselves before their torturers."

Was Crockett one of these "unfortunates"? Lieutenant Peña's diary says so. But one of the widows who survived the battle later said that she'd seen Crockett die very early in the fighting.

Joe, a slave belonging to Colonel Travis and the only male Texan to survive the battle, later said he'd seen Crockett's dead body surrounded by slain Mexican soldiers.

It is a point that may never be settled. But one fact is certain: By nine o'clock that same morning all 189 defenders of the Alamo were dead.

When the battle was over, Santa Anna sent for Francisco Ruiz, the mayor of San Antonio de Bexar. As they picked their way among the bodies Santa Anna ordered Ruiz to identify the corpses of Travis and Bowie. He wanted to be sure—*very sure*—that they were dead.

Santa Anna then ordered his men to burn all of the bodies. They tugged the corpses across the blood-covered plaza and stacked the bodies in piles along with dry brush and branches. They set the human remains on fire.

Santa Anna was delighted by his victory.

His enemies had been crushed! He watched the bodies of the rebels burn but ordered that his own dead soldiers be given proper burial.

However, more than six hundred of his men had been slain in battle—over one third of the general's troops. There was not enough room in the graveyard.

When he heard how many men he'd lost in his attempt to vanquish that handful of Texans, El Presidente shrugged.

"The loss is a small affair," he said.

Colonel Juan Almonte, however, was more disturbed by the loss of life. There were also many seriously wounded men. Many more would die in the next several days.

General Santa Anna reminded his colonel that the army of Mexico had won a great victory that day.

"Another such victory and we are ruined," Colonel Almonte replied grimly.

CHAPTER SEVEN

"Blood Ran into My Shoes"

FOLLOWING THE siege General Santa Anna demanded that the survivors be brought to him. Most of them were women and children. Susanna Dickinson and her baby, Angelina, were two of these survivors.

Susanna's husband, Almaron Dickinson, was the captain in charge of artillery. Susanna had stayed with him in the old mission to help with the cooking and to care for the sick and wounded men.

When the Mexican army finally stormed over the Alamo's battered walls, Captain

Dickinson searched frantically for his wife and baby girl.

"Sue, all is lost!" he cried. "Save yourself and the child."

Mrs. Dickinson never saw her husband alive again. She rushed to the chapel to hide. The wife of rifleman José Losoya was already hiding there, along with her three frightened children. Ana Esparza and her four youngsters were hiding inside as well.

Colonel Juan Almonte, Santa Anna's chief aide, discovered the frightened women and children hiding in the chapel. He ordered them to come out.

"If you want to live, follow me," he told Susanna in English. He then escorted her to General Santa Anna.

As the twenty-two-year-old widow followed her captor a rifle shot rang out. Susanna stumbled. Blood oozed down her leg and soaked through her long skirt.

She had been wounded in the calf of her right leg. To this day no one knows whether it was an accident or if one of the Mexican soldiers shot her intentionally.

Juana Navarro Alsbury, the wife of a doctor, also survived the siege. Her husband had left the Alamo during the siege on an errand for Colonel Travis. He had not returned by the time Santa Anna's men swarmed over the walls. Mrs. Alsbury hid with her baby boy, Alejo, and her teenage sister Gertrudis.

According to the doctor's wife, Mexican soldiers plundered her trunk of personal belongings. A Texan with the last name of Mitchell tried to protect her from the attacking soldiers. They killed him but left Mrs. Alsbury and her baby and sister unharmed.

Andrea Castanon de Villanueva was another survivor of the siege. She is better known as Madam Candelaria. She owned a small hotel in San Antonio de Bexar. She had come to the Alamo with medicine for Jim Bowie, who was so ill everyone feared he would die.

On that fateful morning of March 6, 1836, Madam Candelaria bravely threw herself in front of her dying patient to save him from being killed. Mexican soldiers wounded her in the arm and chin with their bayonets before they killed the ailing Bowie.

Madam Candelaria was also taken prisoner and brought before General Santa Anna. She was horrified by what she saw that morning as she was led across the smoldering compound. The butchered remains of the Alamo defenders were heaped in the courtyard. The number of slain Mexican soldiers seemed too many to count. The moans and cries of the seriously wounded were pitiful.

"Blood ran into my shoes," she recalled.

Two of the other captives were African-American slaves. Their names were Joe and Sam. They had belonged to Colonel Travis and Bowie, respectively. After the battle Santa Anna declared them free men.

The president of Mexico then gallantly gave each woman a blanket and two dollars in silver. He told them to take their children and go home. He promised that his men would not harm them.

But he gave Susanna Dickinson something in addition to the money and blanket.

"Señora Dickinson, deliver this letter to that so-called General Houston in Gonzales," he ordered. "Tell him that all those who defied me at the Alamo are dead."

Mrs. Dickinson and her baby girl left the mission in an oxcart. Joe, Travis's former slave, and a cook named Ben, a free black man, went with them.

They made their way to the town of Gonzales to deliver Santa Anna's letter. They were met by some of Sam Houston's men, who escorted them to the general's camp.

Still limping from the wound in her leg, Mrs. Dickinson stepped forward and solemnly handed General Houston the letter from the president of Mexico. It read:

Citizens! The causes which have conducted to this frontier a part of the Mexican Army are not unknown to you, a parcel of audacious adventurers, maliciously protected by some inhabitants of a neighboring republic dared to invade our territory, with the intention of dividing amongst themselves the fertile lands that are contained in the spacious Department of Texas; and even had the boldness to entertain the idea of reaching the capital of the republic.

It became necessary to check and chastise such enormous daring; and in consequence, some exemplary punishments have already taken place. . . . I am pained to find amongst those adventurers the names of some colonists, to whom had been granted repeated benefits, and who had no motive of complaint against the government of their adopted country.

These ungrateful men must also necessarily suffer the just punishment that the laws and the public vengeance demand. But if we are bound to punish the criminal, we are not the less compelled to protect the innocent. . . .

Bexarians! Return to your homes and dedicate yourselves to your domestic duties. Your city and the fortress of the Alamo are already in possession of the Mexican Army. . . . The Supreme Government has taken you under its protection. . . .

Inhabitants of Texas! . . . The good will have nothing to fear. Fulfill always your duties as Mexican citizens, . . . for I pledge you in the name of the supreme authorities of the nation, and as your fellow citizen and friend, that what has been promised you will be faithfully performed.

—Antonio Lopes de Santa Anna

* * * *

Then Mrs. Dickinson told General Houston the tragic news: All of the brave defenders at the Alamo were dead.

Sam Houston was numb with disbelief. It just wasn't possible! *All* of the Alamo defenders were dead? Big Jim Bowie? Davy Crockett? Travis, too?

"They all died fighting for liberty . . . as ev'ry true Texan should die," Mrs. Dickinson told him. Her voice quivered.

Sam Houston bowed his head and wept.

CHAPTER EIGHT

"Remember the Alamo! Remember Goliad!"

NEWS OF the tragic defeat at the Alamo spread across Texas like wildfire. But a few weeks later the Texans faced yet another disaster in the town of Goliad.

One of President Santa Anna's generals successfully subdued the Texas forces there. He proudly sent word to his commander in chief in San Antonio de Bexar that he had captured more than three hundred Texian prisoners. One of them was Colonel James Fannin.

Santa Anna was pleased. He was also surprised. Had his officers forgotten their orders? Was there not a policy that *all* troublesome rebels were to be put to death?

Annoyed, Santa Anna ordered that all of the Texian prisoners should be shot.

Reluctantly the Mexican officers obeyed the order. At dawn on March 27, 1836, the prisoners were marched in formation. It was Palm Sunday. The unarmed Texians wondered if they were going to be paroled.

Suddenly the entire garrison of Mexican soldiers opened fire. They massacred the helpless Texians by the hundreds. The Mexicans then jerked the clothing off the corpses. They flung the naked bodies into burning piles of brush.

Witnesses declared that even several days after the mass execution hands and feet were still visible in the gruesome pile of ashes.

This brutality fanned the Texians' anger

into a blazing fury! "Remember the Alamo! Remember Goliad!" became their heated battle cry.

Then on April 21, 1836, General Sam Houston and his army got their revenge. The famous Battle of San Jacinto took place in bayou country near present-day Houston. Together, Texians and *Tejanos* attacked Santa Anna and his weary army.

It was late in the afternoon. The Mexicans were taking a siesta. They napped behind a defensive barricade about five feet high. This wall was made using sacks of stale bread, saddlebags, branches, and brush.

The Texans stormed the barricade. Santa Anna's military secretary observed the battle. He saw the grim faces of the Texans. He noted the men's deadly skill with their rifles.

When the fighting was too close for rifles, they fought hand to hand. The angry Texans proved to be as skilled with their knives as they were with their rifles.

They killed scores of Santa Anna's men. The general's military secretary later wrote: "There were an infinite number of dead piled one upon the other, till they might have served as a bridge."

Many of the Mexicans at the rear began to panic. Frantically they killed one another as they tried to flee from the wrath of the Texans. Those who survived the battle later recalled how the Texans had "fought with the fury of demons."

Some of the frightened troops ran to the bridge spanning Vince's Bayou, hoping to escape. But Houston's men had already thought of that possibility and had burned the bridge.

The fleeing Mexican soldiers had no place to run. There was nothing they could do now—except turn back and face the fury of the Texans.

It was a short battle, but a deadly one. In eighteen minutes of fierce fighting eight hundred Texians and *Tejanos* killed more than half of Santa Anna's fifteen hundred troops. The freedom fighters lost only nine men.

Santa Anna was afraid of being captured, tortured, and killed. His own soldiers later recalled that their general had shrieked with fear. El Presidente raced away from the scene of the battle. When his horse got bogged down in the mud near the river, the dictator tried to hide.

Houston's men found him near the river. They didn't know who he was at first. Santa Anna had stripped off his fine general's uniform and put on the plain uniform of a cavalry soldier!

Houston ordered his important prisoner to be bound with chains. Houston then disarmed Santa Anna's surviving men and forced them to retreat to Mexico.

"Don't ever set foot on Texas soil again," he warned them.

Juan Seguín and his company of *Tejanos* made sure the troops marched straight back to Mexico. Later Seguín organized a proper burial for the ashes of the Alamo defenders.

Outraged Texans wanted Santa Anna dead. They could not forget his cruelty at the Alamo and Goliad.

Houston and his men had a difficult time trying to protect their unpopular prisoner. They needed to keep Santa Anna safe until he signed the treaty granting Texas its independence.

Lorenzo de Zavala served as the interpreter and liaison between President Santa

Anna and the new government of Texas. The president of Mexico was then escorted under heavy guard to Washington, D.C., where he was forced to sign the Treaty of Velasco. Texas was free at last!

The United States government promised the new republic its complete support. England, France, and other countries around the world also recognized Texas as a new, independent nation.

Liberty-loving Americans romanticized the story of the siege. Davy Crockett, William Travis, and Jim Bowie were larger-than-life heroes. Sam Houston and Stephen Austin became living legends.

When Texas held its first national election, citizens elected popular Sam Houston as their first president. De Zavala was elected vice president of the new republic. He urged his fellow citizens of Texas to petition to join

the United States of America: "For by this action the stability of our government will be assured and because I believe it will be very difficult for Texas to march alone among the other independent nations."

Most Texans felt the same. In 1845, after only nine years as an independent nation, Texas became the twenty-eighth state to join the Union.

Today the Alamo is known as the Cradle of Texas Liberty. Men and boys are asked to remove their hats respectfully upon entering the old mission. Although the Alamo is small in size, the ideas the men fought and died for are big ones.

It is unlikely that Texans will ever forget "the thirteen days of glory" at the siege of the Alamo.